introduction

Welcome to the Keto Instant Pot Recipes Cookbook! I'm excited to be able to offer you these 60 high-fat, low-carb Instant Pot recipes for an even quicker "fix it and forget it" keto experience that will reduce your stress while you reduce your waistline. You may have used your Instant Pot for tons of meals before, but I promise the recipes you'll find in these pages are going to revamp your keto experience and reignite your love for your Instant Pot.

We've included a special bonus section of keto staples for you, too — most of these are made in the Instant Pot, but some are just great key recipes to have on hand to make keto eating effortless and tasty. With recipes like keto tortillas, homemade ghee, and easy pickled veggies, your keto snacking and cooking will be easy and interesting! You can dress up your meals with wholesome extras that you know will keep you on track with your fat loss.

I'm excited to share this great resource with you, and I hope it supports your keto and Paleo journey. Enjoy the recipes, and I'll see you in the kitchen!

Take care, and be well

Kelsey Ale

-Kelsey

Recipe Photography:

Jennafer Ashley
Tatiana Briceag
Stephanie Goldfinger
Zoe Lyons

Cover Photography: Jennafer Ashley

about me.

Kelsey Ale is a certified Nutritional Therapy Practitioner and Paleo chef/baker living in Santa Monica, California. She discovered her passion for healthy cooking and desserts over 15 years ago. Shortly after, she started running the juice bar at her local health food store where her love for holistic health began to grow. But she still faced severe health challenges of her own. After discovering how the Paleo diet and other natural lifestyle adjustments helped her heal her own body and recover from illness, Kelsey became fully committed to showing the world how to use delicious food to lose weight, increase mental clarity and energy, and achieve vibrant health.

"Follow me on Instagram and Facebook @thekelseyale to get natural health tips, down-to-earth nutrition advice that works, yummy recipes, and more!"

— Kelsey, www.KelseyAle.com

contents.

Staples

Breakfasts

Soups

Mains

Desserts

RECIPE KEY

Measurements

T = Tablespoon
t = teaspoon
oz = ounces
lb = pounds

 **Total:** *

* The time for the pressure to build is not included in this total.

staples.

Country
Cottage
Jars

BEEF BONE BROTH

Prep: 10 mins

Cook: 3 hrs

Total: 3 hrs 10 mins*

Yield: 1 cup

Nutritional info per serving:

Calories	*Carbs*	*Protein*	*Fat*
250	*4g*	*21g*	*14g*

INGREDIENTS:

3-4 lb pasture-raised beef bones, roasted

2 medium carrots, chopped

2 celery stalks, chopped

1 medium onion, sliced in half

2 cloves garlic

8 cups filtered water (or enough to cover bones)

1 t sea salt

1 T apple cider vinegar

METHOD:

Preheat the oven to 400°F, and line a baking sheet with aluminum foil.

Place the bones on the baking sheet, and roast for 40 minutes. Halfway through the cooking time, flip each bone over to roast on the other side. Once the bones are roasted, place them in the Instant Pot.

Chop the vegetables and garlic (no need to peel), and add them to the Instant Pot. You can also add vegetable scraps (such as carrot peel etc.) and vegetable leftovers to the pot because the broth is strained after it's cooked.

Fill the Instant Pot with water until it just covers the contents or the Instant Pot bowl is ⅔ full. Season with 1 teaspoon of sea salt and 1 tablespoon of apple cider vinegar.

Place the lid on the Instant Pot and lock it into place. Move the vent knob to the sealed position. Select "Manual" and cook on low pressure for 3 hours.

Release the pressure using the natural release method. Unlock and remove the lid.

Carefully remove the vegetables and bones with a slotted spoon. Save the bones because they can be used several times. Strain the remaining broth liquid through a fine-mesh strainer, and cool.

Once the broth has fully cooled, remove some of the fat layers that form at the top. These can be discarded or used for cooking.

A good broth will usually gelatinize when thoroughly cool.

Store the bone broth in a Mason jar in the fridge for 3–4 days. (If you have excess bone broth, it's best to store it in the freezer in silicone ice cube trays or a BPA-free plastic container.)

Country
Cottage
Jars

CHICKEN BONE BROTH

Prep: 10 mins

Cook: 2 hrs

Total: 2 hrs 10 mins*

Yield: 8 cups

Yield: 1 cup

Nutritional info per serving:

Calories	Carbs	Protein	Fat
138	4g	25g	2g

INGREDIENTS:

*2 carcasses from roasted chickens or up to 2 lbs chicken bones (*see tip below)*

2 medium carrots, chopped

2 celery stalks, chopped

1 medium onion, chopped

2 cloves garlic

8 cups filtered water (or enough to just cover the contents)

1 t sea salt

1 T apple cider vinegar

**** Tip: Chicken feet are fantastic for bone broth. Ask your butcher for organic unbleached chicken feet to add to your bone broth.***

METHOD:

If using fresh bones, from chickens that haven't been previously roasted, preheat the oven to 400°F, and line a baking sheet with aluminum foil.

Place the bones on the baking sheet, and roast for 40 minutes. Halfway through the cooking time, flip each bone over to roast on the other side.

Once the bones are roasted, place them in the Instant Pot.

Chop the vegetables and garlic (no need to peel), and add them to the Instant Pot. You can also add vegetable scraps (such as carrot peel etc.) and vegetable leftovers to the pot because the broth is strained after it's cooked.

Fill the Instant Pot with water until it just covers the contents or the Instant Pot bowl is ⅔ full. Season with 1 teaspoon of sea salt and 1 tablespoon of apple cider vinegar.

Place the lid on the Instant Pot and lock it into place. Move the vent knob to the sealed position. Select "Manual" and cook on low pressure for 2 hours (or you can cook on high pressure for 75 minutes.)

Release the pressure using the natural release method. Unlock and remove the lid.

Carefully remove the vegetables and bones with a slotted spoon, strain the remaining broth liquid through a fine-mesh strainer, and cool.

Once the broth has fully cooled, you'll be able to remove some of the fat layers that form at the top, which you can discard or use for cooking. A good broth will usually gelatinize when thoroughly cool.

Store the bone broth in a Mason jar in the fridge for 3–4 days. (If you have excess bone broth, it's best to store it in the freezer in silicone ice cube trays or a BPA-free plastic container.)

CAULIFLOWER RICE

Prep: 5 mins

Cook: 5 mins

Total: 10 mins*

Yield: 4 servings

Nutritional info per serving:

Calories	Carbs	Protein	Fat
97	7g	3g	7g

INGREDIENTS:

1 head cauliflower, stems removed, and cut into small florets

*1 T **optional seasonings:** sea salt, garlic, ginger, coconut aminos, curry, garlic, or freshly ground black pepper*

2 T coconut oil or ghee

½ t salt, to taste

¼ t black pepper, to taste

METHOD:

Place the raw cauliflower florets into a food processor, and pulse several times, until it has a grainy, rice-like consistency. Season with sea salt, freshly ground black pepper, and any additional seasonings if desired. Set aside.

Set the Instant Pot on saute mode and add the coconut oil to the pot. When melted, add the riced cauliflower and stir for 1–2 minutes, until the "rice" starts to soften.

Press cancel and transfer the cauliflower rice to an oven-safe bowl that will fit into the inner pot of the Instant Pot.

Add 1½ cups water to the inner pot (there's no need to wash the bits of leftover cauliflower out of it) and place a trivet at the bottom. Place the bowl with the cauliflower rice on the trivet.

Secure the Instant Pot lid and move the vent knob to the sealed position.

Set the Instant Pot to "Manual" and cook on high pressure for 5 minutes.

Quickly release the pressure and remove the lid.

Add salt and pepper, seasoning to taste.

CAULIFLOWER MASHED POTATOES

Prep: 5 mins

Cook: 4 mins

Total: 9 mins*

Yield: 4 servings

Nutritional info per serving:

Calories	Carbs	Protein	Fat
71	8g	3g	4g

INGREDIENTS:

1 large head cauliflower

1 T ghee, coconut oil or olive oil

¼ t sea salt

¼ t black pepper

¼ t garlic powder

1 T chopped chives for garnish, optional

METHOD:

Place a steamer rack or trivet with handles in the bowl of the Instant Pot, and add the water.

Remove the core and cut the cauliflower into large pieces.

Place the cauliflower on the trivet, and secure the lid on the Instant Pot. Move the vent knob to the sealed position.

Select "Manual" and cook for 4 minutes on high pressure.

Carefully open the vent to quickly release the pressure.

Open the lid and remove the trivet and cauliflower. Drain the water and place the cauliflower back into the inner bowl.

Add the ghee, salt, pepper, and garlic powder, and puree using an immersion blender.

Garnish with chives if desired.

SPAGHETTI SQUASH NOODLES

Prep: 3 mins

Cook: 7 mins

Total: 10 mins*

Yield: 4 servings

Nutritional info per serving:

Calories	*Carbs*	*Protein*	*Fat*
56	*5g*	*2g*	*4g*

INGREDIENTS:

1 (2 lb) spaghetti squash

METHOD:

Place 1½ cups water and a steamer rack or trivet with handles in the inner bowl of the Instant Pot.

Add 1 cup of water to the Instant Pot. Place a trivet in the pot. Place the squash on top of the trivet and secure the lid.

Move the vent knob to the sealed position and cook on high pressure for 15 minutes.

Carefully open the vent to quickly release the pressure.

Remove the squash from the pot and when cool enough to handle, slice the squash in half and remove the seeds.

Shred the squash flesh with a fork.

ZUCCHINI NOODLES

Prep: 15 mins

Cook: 3 mins

Total: 18 mins*

Yield: 4 servings

Nutritional info per serving:

Calories	*Carbs*	*Protein*	*Fat*
56	*5g*	*2g*	*4g*

INGREDIENTS:

3 medium zucchini

1 T avocado oil

Sea salt and pepper, to taste

METHOD:

If using a peeler, make long peels down the length of the zucchini.

If using a spiralizer, follow the instructions of the spiralizer to make zucchini noodles.

For the best, least-watery results, sprinkle the noodles with a little salt, then press them between paper towels, and let sit for 10–15 minutes. Pat with a paper towel one more time before cooking.

Select "Saute" on the Instant Pot and place the zoodles in the pot with the avocado oil. Saute for 2–3 minutes or until the zoodles become tender.

Sprinkle salt and pepper over the zoodles, stir once more, and serve as a side or with your favorite sauce.

PICKLED VEGGIES

Prep: 5 mins

Cook: 1 hr

Total: 1 hr 5 mins*

Yield: 2 lbs pickled veg (~16 servings)

Serving Size: 2 oz

Nutritional info per serving:

Calories	Carbs	Protein	Fat
18	4g	1g	0g

INGREDIENTS:

1 cup water

2 cups apple cider vinegar

1½ T sea salt

1 t black peppercorns

3 garlic cloves, peeled

*3 Persian cucumbers, sliced in half lengthwise***

1 lb peeled carrots, chopped into sticks

1 medium onion, sliced into ¼-inch slices

***Note: You can pick your own combination of low-starch veggies like cauliflower, radishes, etc to make this mixture exactly what you want!*

METHOD:

Combine the water, vinegar, salt, peppercorns, and garlic in the bowl of the Instant Pot. Secure the lid and move the vent knob to the sealed position.

Select "Manual" and cook on high pressure for 1 minute.

While the Instant Pot is pressurizing, distribute the veggies into containers or jars with lids, such as Mason jars.

When the cooking time is up, carefully move the vent knob to "Venting" for quick pressure release.

Remove the Instant Pot lid and pour the vinegar mixture into the jars to cover the veggies.

Allow to cool for at least an hour before eating (the pickling will be partially done at this point), or close the lids and store in the refrigerator. The veggies will be completely pickled in 24 hours.

KETO TORTILLAS

Prep: 10 mins

Cook: 12 mins

Total: 22 mins*

Yield: 6 tortillas

Serving Size: 1 tortilla

Nutritional info per serving:

Calories	Carbs	Protein	Fat
88	6g	2g	6g

INGREDIENTS:

1 cup almond flour

4 T ground psyllium husks

½ t baking powder

1 t salt

¼ cup boiling water

1 large egg

1 T avocado oil

METHOD:

Combine the almond flour, psyllium husks, baking powder, and salt in a medium mixing bowl, and mix well to combine.

Add the boiling water, and mix well.

Add the egg and mix well until completely combined, then allow the dough to rest for a few minutes while you prepare 2 sheets of parchment paper on the counter.

Divide the dough into 6 golf-ball-sized pieces.

Roll out the dough between the 2 pieces of parchment paper until they are ⅛-inch thick and about 4 to 5-inch circles across. Don't make them too big or thin, or they will stick to the parchment.

Select "Saute" on the Instant Pot and heat the avocado oil until hot but not smoking, 30 seconds to 1 minute.*

Add the first tortilla and cook until done on the first side, about 1 minute. Flip, and cook an additional minute on the second side, then remove it from the heat and set aside on a plate. Repeat with the remaining tortillas, adding additional oil as needed.

Store the tortillas in an airtight container in the fridge for up to 5 days. Enjoy!

*Alternatively, for the ease of cooking on a flat surface, you can cook your tortillas in a pan on the stove.

KETO BUNS

Prep: 5 mins

Cook: 12 mins

Total: 17 mins*

Yield: 4 servings

Serving Size: 1 bun

Nutritional info per serving:

Calories	*Carbs*	*Protein*	*Fat*
134	*2g*	*7g*	*11g*

INGREDIENTS:

4 large eggs

4 t olive oil plus more for greasing ramekins

½ cup almond meal

¼ t salt

1 T dried oregano, divided

METHOD:

Place 1½ cups water and a steamer rack or trivet in the Instant Pot Bowl.

Grease 4 (6-ounce) ramekins.

In a large bowl, beat the eggs and olive oil.

Sift the almond meal, salt, and 2½ teaspoons of dried oregano into the egg mixture. Whisk well.

Divide the batter between the 4 ramekins, then sprinkle the remaining oregano on top of the batter.

Secure the lid on the Instant Pot and move the vent knob to the sealed position. Select "Manual" and cook on high pressure for 12 minutes. Let the pressure release naturally for 5 minutes, then carefully open the vent to release the rest of the pressure quickly.

Remove the ramekins from the Instant Pot and when cool enough to touch, run a knife around the edges of the buns and slip them onto a serving dish. Serve warm or cold.

GHEE

Prep: 5 mins

Cook: 10 mins

Rest: 10 mins

Total: 25 mins*

Yield: 1 cup (16 servings)

Serving Size: 1 T each

Nutritional info per serving:

Calories	Carbs	Protein	Fat
89	0g	0g	9g

INGREDIENTS:

1 lb unsalted organic, grass-fed butter

METHOD:

Place the butter in the bowl of the Instant Pot and turn on the "Saute" setting.

Cook undisturbed for 7 minutes until three layers form: the milk solid foam at the top, the clear butter oil layer in the middle, and the milk solids at the bottom of the pot.

Start watching the butter carefully at the 7-minute mark and press "Cancel" on the Instant Pot when the milk solids on the bottom caramelize to a golden brown color. This should be somewhere between 8–10 minutes.

When the ghee is ready, remove the inner pot from the base to prevent further heating and place it on a cooling rack or a towel.

Let the ghee cool for 10 minutes and then remove and discard the foamy top layer with a spoon.

Carefully strain the remaining ghee from the pot through a cheesecloth into a clean, sterile Mason jar. Discard the brown pieces that have been strained.

Place in the refrigerator to set for at least 20 minutes.

Keep the ghee refrigerated in between uses. A jar of refrigerated ghee will last up to 1 year.

breakfast.

SHAKSHUKA

Prep: 5 mins

Cook: 11 mins

Total: 16 mins*

Yield: 4 servings

Nutritional info per serving:

Calories	Carbs	Protein	Fat
186	10g	8g	13g

INGREDIENTS:

2 T ghee

½ cup chopped green bell peppers

¼ cup chopped white onion

1 t minced garlic

1 t ground cumin

1 t dried oregano

½ t sea salt

2 cups canned, diced tomatoes in juice

4 large eggs

METHOD:

Put the Instant Pot on saute mode, and melt the ghee.

Add the bell peppers and onion. Saute for 2 minutes until fragrant. Add the garlic, cumin, oregano, sea salt, and tomatoes and stir well.

Secure the lid and move the vent knob to the sealed position. Select "Manual" and cook on high pressure for 10 minutes.

When the cooking is finished, use the quick release and remove the lid.

Make 4 small wells in the tomato mixture with a spoon, and gently drop in the eggs. The easiest way to do this is to crack an egg into a small bowl and slide it into a well. Repeat for each egg.

Lock the lid back into place, move the knob to the sealed position, and cook on high pressure for an additional 1 minute. Carefully move the vent knob to "Venting" for quick pressure release.

Serve hot.

CREAMY COCONUT PORRIDGE

Prep: 5 mins

Cook: 4 mins

Total: 9 mins*

Yield: 2 servings

Nutritional info per serving:

Calories	*Carbs*	*Protein*	*Fat*
416	*11g*	*11g*	*39g*

INGREDIENTS:

1¼ cups full-fat coconut milk

⅓ cup shredded coconut

¼ cup coconut flour

3 T ground flax seed

1 T collagen protein powder

¼ t monk fruit powder

½ t vanilla extract

½ t cinnamon, optional

Optional: Berries, nuts, and seeds for toppings

METHOD:

Pour the coconut milk into the bowl of the Instant Pot. Add the remaining ingredients and stir to combine.

Lock the lid into place and move the vent knob to the sealed position. Set mode to manual and cook on high pressure for 4 minutes.

Use the quick release, remove the lid, and stir the contents thoroughly.

Serve warm with optional toppings.

BREAKFAST SAUSAGE CASSEROLE

Prep: 10 mins

Cook: 42 mins

Total: 52 mins*

Yield: 4 servings

Nutritional info per serving:

Calories	Carbs	Protein	Fat
404	5g	17g	36g

INGREDIENTS:

2 T ghee or coconut oil plus more for greasing the baking dish

6 oz breakfast or mild Italian sausage

1½ cups broccoli slaw (or 3 medium broccoli stalks, grated)

2 garlic cloves, minced

½ t sea salt

¼ t ground black pepper

6 large eggs

¼ cup coconut cream or full-fat coconut milk

1 green onion, thinly sliced

1 avocado, thinly sliced, optional

METHOD:

Grease a 6- or 7-inch casserole dish or springform pan. If using a springform pan, wrap the bottom with foil to prevent leakage. Set aside.

Turn the Instant Pot to "Saute" mode and cook the sausage in the ghee until most of the pink has gone (about 3–4 minutes).

Add the broccoli slaw, garlic, salt, and pepper and saute for 2 minutes.

Press "Cancel" on the Instant Pot and transfer the mixture to the prepared dish.

In a medium bowl, whisk together the eggs and the coconut cream. Stir in the green onion.

Pour the egg mixture into the baking dish on top of the sausage, and cover tightly with foil.

Pour 1½ cups of water into the Instant Pot, and place a steamer rack or trivet on the bottom.

Put the casserole on the trivet and secure the Instant Pot lid. Move the vent knob to the sealed position and cook on "Manual" high pressure for 35 minutes.

When the cooking time is up, release the pressure naturally for 10 minutes and then carefully open the vent to release the rest of the pressure.

Remove the casserole from the Instant Pot. Slice and serve topped with fresh avocado.

"CHEESY" EGG AND BACON BAKE

Prep: 5 mins

Cook: 20 mins

Total: 25 mins*

Yield: 4 servings

Nutritional info per serving:

Calories	Carbs	Protein	Fat
192	3g	15g	13g

INGREDIENTS:

Coconut oil for greasing pan

6 slices bacon, diced

2 cups kale leaves

6 large eggs

¼ cup full-fat coconut milk

¼ cup nutritional yeast

¼ t sea salt

¼ t ground black pepper

METHOD:

Grease a 6- or 7-inch heat-proof bowl or baking dish. Set aside.

Select "Saute" on the Instant Pot and cook the diced bacon until crispy, 5–8 minutes depending on the thickness of your bacon.

While the bacon is cooking, in a medium bowl, whisk the eggs with the coconut milk, nutritional yeast, salt, and pepper. Set aside.

Stir the kale into the bacon about 2 minutes before it's crisped to your liking, and then press "Cancel."

Pour the egg mixture into the prepared baking dish and, using a slotted spoon, add the bacon and kale. Cover with foil.

Remove the excess bacon fat from the Instant Pot bowl and discard, or save for another use. Place a steamer rack or trivet into the bowl (there is no need to wash the bowl first) and add 1½ cups water. Place the dish containing the egg mixture onto the rack and secure the lid.

Select "Manual" and cook on high pressure for 20 minutes. When the cooking time is up, move the vent knob to "Venting" to release the pressure.

After removing the egg bake from the Instant Pot, slice into pieces, and serve.

SPINACH FRITTATA

Prep: 10 mins

Cook: 12 mins

Total: 22 mins*

Yield: 4 servings

Nutritional info per serving:

Calories	Carbs	Protein	Fat
186	2g	13g	14g

INGREDIENTS:

Ghee or coconut oil for greasing the baking dish

8 large eggs

⅓ cup coconut cream or full-fat coconut milk

¾ t sea salt

½ t ground black pepper

½ t chili powder, or to taste

¼ cup bell pepper, diced

¼ cup red onion, minced

½ cup fresh spinach, chopped

***Optional:** chopped green onion, sliced jalapeno pepper, sliced avocado*

METHOD:

In a medium bowl, beat the eggs, coconut cream, salt, pepper, and chili powder together until fluffy.

Add the bell pepper, onion, spinach, and stir to combine.

Pour the mixture into a 6- or 7-inch ceramic baking dish or a springform pan. If using a springform pan, wrap the bottom with foil to prevent leakage.

Pour 1½ cups water into the Instant Pot bowl and place a steamer rack or trivet in the bottom of the pot.

Place the frittata on the rack and secure the lid. Move the vent knob to the sealed position and cook on "Manual" high pressure for 12 minutes.

Let the pressure release naturally for 15 minutes then carefully open the vent to release the rest of the pressure quickly.

Remove the casserole from the Instant Pot.

When cool enough to handle, slice, and serve with your desired toppings.

SPANISH TORTILLA OMELET

Prep: 10 mins

Cook: 12 mins

Total: 22 mins*

Yield: 8 servings

Nutritional info per serving:

Calories	Carbs	Protein	Fat
127	1g	7g	11g

INGREDIENTS:

8 large eggs

2 T nutritional yeast flakes

⅓ cup coconut cream

1 t sea salt

⅛ t black pepper

¼ cup white onion, peeled and thinly sliced

½ cup radishes, peeled and thinly, sliced

½ cup chopped spinach

2 T virgin olive oil

***Optional:** Top with sliced avocado, diced tomato, minced chives, or spring onion*

METHOD:

In a medium bowl beat the eggs, nutritional yeast, and coconut cream together until fluffy. Season with salt and pepper.

Line a 7-inch ceramic baking dish, and brush with olive oil.

Layer the sliced onion, radishes, and spinach. Pour the egg-coconut cream mixture over the layered vegetables.

Place 1 cup of water in the bottom of the Instant Pot, add the steamer rack to the pot and place the ceramic dish on top of the rack. Move the vent knob to the sealed position and cook on "Manual" high pressure for 12 minutes.

Let the pressure release naturally for 15 minutes then carefully open the vent to release the rest of the pressure quickly.

Remove the dish from the pot and invert it onto a serving platter.

Top the Spanish omelet with all of the toppings and serve.

BREAKFAST CREPES

Prep: 10 mins

Cook: 15 mins

Total: 25 mins*

Yield: 2 servings

Nutritional info per serving:

Calories	Carbs	Protein	Fat
376	7g	14g	33g

INGREDIENTS:

¼ cup almond flour

2 T coconut flour

¼ t salt

4 large eggs

⅓ cup canned coconut milk, room temperature

2 T coconut oil or ghee, for cooking

***Optional:** Sugar-free maple syrup for drizzling*

METHOD:

Combine the almond flour, coconut flour, salt, and eggs in a blender and mix until smooth.

Add the room temperature coconut milk. Blend until smooth.

Let the batter rest for about 5 minutes to finish absorbing any extra liquid.

Select "Saute" on the Instant Pot and heat the coconut oil until hot but not smoking (about 30 seconds to a minute*).

Add approximately 2 tablespoons plus a bit more batter to the Instant Pot and cook until done on the first side (about 1 minute). Flip and cook an additional minute on the second side, then remove it from the heat and set aside on a plate.

Repeat with the remaining pancake batter, adding extra oil as needed.

Serve with coconut yogurt and fresh berries. Drizzle with sugar-free maple syrup.

*Alternatively, for the ease of cooking on a flat surface, cook the pancakes in a pan on the stove.

GIANT INSTANT POT PANCAKE

Prep: 5 mins

Cook: 45 mins

Total: 50 mins*

Yield: 4 servings

Nutritional info per serving:

Calories	Carbs	Protein	Fat
288	6g	8g	25g

INGREDIENTS:

1 T coconut oil for greasing the pot

2 eggs

1½ cups full-fat coconut milk

2 cups almond flour

1 T coconut flour

¾ t baking soda

1 t lemon juice

¼ t pure monk fruit powder

METHOD:

Grease the bottom and 2–3 inches of the sides of the inner pot with the coconut oil. Make sure there is a very generous amount on the bottom.

In a large bowl, whisk the eggs and coconut milk until blended. Add the remaining ingredients and whisk until smooth, with just a few small lumps remaining.

Pour the batter into the pot and secure the lid. Move the vent knob to the sealed position.

Select "Manual" and cook on low pressure for 50 minutes. Due to the low pressure and lack of liquid, the Instant Pot may not seal but this is fine, the pancake will cook anyway.

When the cooking time is up, move the vent knob to "Venting" to release the pressure quickly.

Using a spatula, loosen the pancake from the sides of the pan and cut it into 4 wedges. Lift the wedges out of the pot and flip them onto a serving plate with the golden brown side up.

Serve with your favorite keto pancake toppings

KETO GRANOLA

Prep: 10 mins

Cook: 2 hrs

Total: 2 hrs 10 mins*

Yield: 12 servings

Nutritional info per serving:

Calories	*Carbs*	*Protein*	*Fat*
354	*10g*	*18g*	*35g*

INGREDIENTS:

¼ cup coconut oil, melted

1 t vanilla stevia, liquid

½ cup chopped almonds

½ cup chopped walnuts

½ cup chopped pecans

½ cup chopped cashews

1 cup sunflower seeds

1 cup pumpkin seeds

1 cup unsweetened shredded coconut

½ cup erythritol

1 t ground cinnamon

½ t salt

METHOD:

This recipe uses the Slow Cooker function on the Instant Pot.

Spray the inside of the Instant Pot with coconut oil cooking spray.

Pour in the nuts, seeds, shredded coconut, erythritol, cinnamon, and salt. Mix.

In a small bowl, whisk together the melted coconut oil and stevia.

Pour the wet ingredients over the dry ingredients and mix until fully combined.

Cover and cook on LOW for 2 hours, stirring every 30 minutes, until you can smell the nuts and the granola begins to brown.

Pour the granola on a parchment-lined baking sheet, and spread it into an even layer to cool for 1–2 hours. (This is also how it will crisp up!)

Store in a covered container and enjoy!

INSTANT POT COCONUT YOGURT

Prep: 5 mins

Cook: 24 hrs

Chill: 4-6 hrs

Rest: 30 mins

Total: 30 hrs*

Yield: 5 servings

Nutritional info per serving:

Calories	Carbs	Protein	Fat
285	9g	3g	28g

INGREDIENTS:

*2 cans full-fat coconut milk**

*1 package yogurt starter with live cultures***

1 T gelatin

***Optional:** Fresh or frozen berries, Keto Granola (recipe page 39), or your favorite keto mix-ins*

***Tip:** You can also use canned coconut cream such as 365 Organic Coconut Cream.*

*****Note:** We recommend Cultures for Health Vegan Yogurt Starter Culture. https://amzn.to/36B5M5f*

METHOD:

Sterilize all of the cooking utensils and the Instant Pot bowl by rinsing with boiling water or sterilizing in the dishwasher.

Pour the coconut milk into the bowl of the Instant Pot, select "Saute," and bring the milk to boil. There is no need for a lid at this stage.

When the milk has reached a boil, press cancel and remove the bowl to a cooling rack. Whisk in the gelatin and let the mixture cool on the counter for about 30 minutes until the temperature comes down to between 100 –110°F. (It's important to use a thermometer to make sure the temperature is in this range because if the yogurt is too hot, it will kill the probiotic cultures.)

Speed up the cooling process by submerging the bottom of the bowl in a larger bowl filled with ice water. This will cool the milk down in a few minutes.

When the correct temperature is reached, whisk in the yogurt starter until fully incorporated.

At this point, you can pour the coconut milk into ramekins, jars, or Instant Pot yogurt cups. Or you can leave the yogurt in the bowl and transfer it to serving cups after it sets up.

With the bowl back in the Instant Pot, secure the lid and select "Yogurt." Adjust the time to a minimum of 8 hours, and up to 24 hours. The longer the fermentation process, the tangier the yogurt. Don't wait for it to thicken, as this will happen when refrigerated.

When the fermentation time is up, open the lid, and taste the yogurt. If you prefer it tangier, ferment it for up to an additional 12 hours (36 hours total). When the yogurt is tangy enough, pour it into cups or jars and add any desired toppings. Chill in the refrigerator for 4–6 hours to thicken. Enjoy!

Soups.

ZUPPA TOSCANA

Prep: 5 mins

Cook: 20 mins

Total: 25 mins*

Yield: 6 servings

Nutritional info per serving:

Calories	*Carbs*	*Protein*	*Fat*
400	*9g*	*24g*	*30g*

INGREDIENTS:

2 strips pasture-raised bacon

1 lb ground pork

1 t ground fennel

1 t minced garlic

½ t dried oregano

½ t dried basil

¼ t red pepper flakes

1 t sea salt

6 cups chicken bone broth (recipe page 3)

½ cup chopped white onion

3 cups cauliflower florets

3 cups chopped kale

1 cup coconut cream

METHOD:

Cut the bacon into 1-inch pieces. Set the Instant Pot to saute mode and cook the bacon for 6-8 minutes or until cooked through, turning frequently to prevent burning. Use tongs to remove the bacon and set aside, leaving the drippings in the pot.

Add the ground pork, fennel, garlic, oregano, basil, pepper flakes, and sea salt to the drippings and brown the pork for about 8 minutes, using a spatula to break it up into crumbles. Stir occasionally.

Using a spoon, remove the excess grease from the pan if desired.

Add the chicken bone broth, onions, cauliflower florets, and kale to the Instant Pot. Lock the lid into place, and move the vent knob to the sealed position. Select "Manual" or "Soup" and cook on high pressure for 3 minutes.

Use either the quick release or natural release and remove the lid. Press "Cancel" and select "Saute." Stir in the coconut cream and bacon, and cook until warmed through (about 1 minute).

CLAM CHOWDER

Prep: 10 mins

Cook: 12 mins

Total: 22 mins*

Yield: 4 servings

Nutritional info per serving:

Calories	Carbs	Protein	Fat
398	10g	18g	29g

INGREDIENTS:

3 oz bacon, diced

½ onion, chopped

2 (6.5 oz) cans clams, chopped finely, keep the clam liquid

*1 lb jicama (cut into small pieces)***

1 cup chicken bone broth (recipe page 3)

1 t sea salt to taste

¼ t pepper

1½ cups full-fat coconut cream or coconut milk

***Optional:** Garnish each serving with a sprinkling of chopped fresh parsley.*

*****Note:** Cauliflower can be substituted instead of jicama.*

METHOD:

Select "Saute" on the Instant Pot and cook the bacon and onion until the bacon is crispy and the onion is translucent (about 8 minutes).

Press "Cancel" and add the clams and their liquid, jicama pieces, and chicken bone broth. Season with salt and pepper to taste.

Lock the lid into place and move the vent knob to the sealed position. Select "Soup" or "Manual" and cook on high pressure for 3 minutes. When the time is up, select "Cancel."

Use either the quick release or natural release and remove the lid. (If you prefer a thicker soup, you can puree part of it including the broth and jicama pieces, and return the puree to the Instant Pot.)

Select saute mode and stir in the coconut cream. Cook until warmed through (about 1 minute).

Taste and season by adding more salt and pepper, as needed.

Top each serving with a sprinkling of chopped fresh parsley, and enjoy!

GREEN CHILE CHICKEN CHOWDER

Prep: 15 mins

Cook: 20 mins

Total: 35 mins*

Yield:6 servings

Nutritional info per serving:

Calories	*Carbs*	*Protein*	*Fat*
210	*10g*	*18g*	*11g*

INGREDIENTS:

1 lb frozen cauliflower florets

2 cups chicken bone broth (recipe on page 3), divided

2 T ghee or other cooking fat

2½ cups peeled and diced celeriac root

1½ cups diced onion

1½ t sea salt

¼ t ground pepper

1½ t ground cumin

1 t garlic powder

¾ t dried oregano

½ t chipotle powder

1 lb boneless, skinless chicken thighs

⅓ cup salsa verde (no sugar added)

1 (4oz) can diced green chiles

1 lime, juiced and zested

¼ cup diced fresh cilantro

METHOD:

Add the cauliflower and ½ cup of the broth to the Instant Pot.

Place the lid on the Instant Pot and lock it in place. Move the vent knob to the sealed position.

Select "Manual" and cook on high pressure for 2 minutes. Once the cooking time is up, press "Cancel" and carefully move the vent knob to release the pressure quickly.

Transfer the cooked cauliflower and broth to a blender, and blend until smooth. Set aside.

Select "Saute" on the Instant Pot, and add the ghee to the bits of cauliflower left in the pot. Heat until the ghee is melted and starting to bubble.

Add the celeriac root, onion, salt, pepper, cumin, garlic powder, oregano, chipotle powder, and saute until the celeriac and onions start to soften(about 3-4 minutes).

Add the chicken thighs and broth, and stir to combine.

Secure the lid on the Instant Pot and move the vent knob to the sealed position.

Select "Manual" and cook on high pressure for 13 minutes.

Once the cooking time is up, release the steam naturally or carefully move the vent knob to "Venting" for a quick pressure release. Leave the Instant Pot in warm mode.

Using tongs or a slotted spoon, carefully remove the chicken from the pot and shred with 2 forks.

Add the chicken back to the pot along with the cauliflower mixture, salsa verde, green chilis, lime juice, and zest and stir to combine.

Serve topped with chopped fresh cilantro.

HUNGARIAN GOULASH

Prep: 5 mins

Cook: 35 mins

Total: 40 mins*

Yield: 6 servings

Nutritional info per serving:

Calories	*Carbs*	*Protein*	*Fat*
275	*7g*	*28g*	*13g*

INGREDIENTS:

2 T almond flour

1 T water

2 T cooking fat, divided

2 lbs stew beef, cut into 1-inch cubes, divided

1 t sea salt, divided

½ t black ground pepper, divided

1 medium onion, chopped

2 bell peppers, chopped

1 t garlic, minced

1 t caraway seed

2 T paprika

2 cups beef bone broth (recipe page 1)

1 cup crushed tomatoes

3 T red wine, optional

Fresh parsley

METHOD:

In a small bowl, mix the almond flour and water together to form a paste. Set aside.

Select "Saute" mode on the Instant Pot and heat half the cooking fat until warm, but not smoking.

Place half the beef cubes in the pot and season with half the salt and pepper. Brown on all sides for 3–4 minutes. With a slotted spoon, remove the beef from the pot and set aside. Repeat with the remaining beef.

After all the beef has been removed from the pot, add the remaining cooking fat to the juices in the pot and saute the onion and bell pepper until soft (about 3 minutes).

Stir in the garlic, caraway seed, paprika, and cook for 1 minute.

Press cancel, and add the beef back to the pot, along with the broth, tomatoes, wine (if using), and the almond flour mixture. Stir to combine all the ingredients.

Secure the lid on the Instant Pot, and move the vent knob to the sealed position.

Select "Stew" or "Manual" and cook on high pressure for 25 minutes.

Once the cooking time is up, release the steam naturally.

Serve with fresh parsley.

Tip: For a thicker sauce, let the goulash simmer on "Saute" mode, uncovered, for 15–30 minutes.

CHICKEN FAJITA SOUP

Prep: 10 mins

Cook: 12 mins

Total: 22 mins*

Yield: 6 servings

Nutritional info per serving:

Calories	*Carbs*	*Protein*	*Fat*
261	*9g*	*20g*	*16g*

INGREDIENTS:

1 T coconut oil

1 bell pepper, seeded and sliced

1 small onion chopped

3 T taco seasoning

1½ cups crushed tomatoes

1 cup chicken bone broth (recipe page 3)

1½ lb chicken thighs

***Optional toppings:** avocado, diced red onion, diced tomatoes, chopped green onions, sliced jalapenos, chopped cilantro*

METHOD:

Add the coconut oil to the Instant Pot. Select "Saute" and cook the bell pepper and onion until starting to soften (about 3 minutes).

Add the taco seasoning and cook for 1 minute. Add the tomatoes, broth, and chicken thighs and stir to combine.

Secure the lid on the Instant Pot and move the vent knob to the sealed position.

Select "Soup" or "Manual" and cook on high pressure for 12 minutes.

Once the cooking time is up, release the pressure naturally or carefully move the vent knob to "Venting" for quick pressure release.

Shred the chicken with 2 forks.

Serve garnished with your favorite toppings.

CHICKEN ENCHILADA SOUP

Prep: 10 mins

Cook: 20 mins

Total: 30 mins*

Yield: 4 servings

Nutritional info per serving:

Calories	*Carbs*	*Protein*	*Fat*
239	*9g*	*29g*	*7g*

INGREDIENTS:

1 T avocado oil

1 small onion, diced

1 red bell pepper, chopped

1 jalapeño pepper, seeded and minced

3 cloves garlic, minced

1 (8 oz) can tomato sauce, no sugar added

1 T chili powder

1 T chipotle pepper in adobo sauce

2 t ground cumin

1 t garlic powder

1 t onion powder

1 t apple cider vinegar

¾ t sea salt, or to taste

½ t oregano

3 cups chicken bone broth (recipe page 3)

1 lb chicken breasts

***Optional toppings:** diced avocado, jalapeno pepper slices, minced cilantro*

METHOD:

Select "Saute" on the Instant Pot and heat the avocado oil until hot but not smoking (about 30-60 seconds).

Add the onion, bell pepper, and jalapeño pepper and cook until soft (about 3 minutes). Add the garlic and cook for another minute.

Add the tomato sauce, chili powder, chipotle pepper, cumin, garlic powder, onion powder, apple cider vinegar, salt, and oregano. Stir to combine.

Press "Cancel," and add the bone broth and chicken.

Secure the Instant Pot lid and move the vent knob to the sealed position. Select "Manual" and cook on high pressure for 20 minutes. When the cooking time is up, carefully move the vent knob to "Venting" to release the pressure quickly.

Remove the chicken to a cutting board and shred with two forks, then return the chicken to the pot and stir into the sauce.

Serve with desired toppings.

SPICY BEEF AND ZOODLE SOUP

Prep: 10 mins

Cook: 8 mins

Total: 18 mins*

Yield: 6 servings

Nutritional info per serving:

Calories	*Carbs*	*Protein*	*Fat*
305	*8g*	*29g*	*17g*

INGREDIENTS:

2 T avocado oil

1½ lbs top sirloin, cut into bite-sized pieces

3 T fresh ginger, minced

2 cloves garlic, chopped

8 oz Bella mushrooms, sliced

6 cups beef bone broth (recipe page 1)

¼ cup apple cider vinegar

¼ cup coconut aminos

¼ cup sriracha

1 large zucchini, spiralized (about 3–4 cups)

Sea salt and ground black pepper to taste

***Optional:** 2 cups of your favorite veggies, such as cauliflower, broccoli, and bok choy*

***Garnish:** ⅓ cup chopped green onion*

METHOD:

Select "Saute" on the Instant Pot and heat the avocado oil. When hot, add the beef, ginger, and garlic and cook for 3–5 minutes until the beef is lightly browned on all sides. Select "Cancel."

Add the mushrooms, broth, vinegar, coconut aminos, and sriracha. Add the veggies. Or, if you prefer a crispier result, add them after the pressure cooking.

Stir and secure the lid. Move the vent knob to the sealed position and cook for 8 minutes on high pressure. When the cooking time is up, move the knob to "Venting" to quickly release the pressure. Press "Cancel."

Remove the lid and stir in the zucchini. Season with salt and pepper, and garnish individual servings with green onion.

ITALIAN SAUSAGE SOUP

Prep: 5 mins

Cook: 10 mins

Total: 15 mins*

Yield: 4 servings

Nutritional info per serving:

Calories	Carbs	Protein	Fat
388	10g	39g	21g

INGREDIENTS:

1 T avocado oil or cooking fat of choice

1 lb Italian sausage, casings removed

1 medium onion, diced

3 cloves garlic, minced

1 t dried oregano

¼ cup sundried tomatoes, drained and chopped

6 cups chicken bone broth (recipe page 3)

1 bunch (4 cups) kale leaves, stems removed, chopped into bite-sized pieces

¾ cup coconut cream

Sea salt and ground black pepper, to taste

***Optional:** ¼ nutritional yeast for a "cheesy" finish and chopped parsley for garnish*

METHOD:

Select "Saute" on the Instant Pot and cook the sausage in the oil until lightly browned (about 4-5 minutes). Drain the excess fat if desired, and add the onion and garlic. Saute for 2-3 minutes until the onion is softened and fragrant.

Press "Cancel" and add the oregano, sundried tomatoes, and broth. Stir to combine.

Secure the Instant Pot lid and move the vent knob to the sealed position.

Press "Manual" and cook on high pressure for 5 minutes. When the cooking time is up, move the vent knob to "Venting" to quickly release the pressure.

Remove the lid and select "Saute" mode. Stir in the kale and coconut cream.

Season with salt and pepper to taste.

Serve hot and garnish with nutritional yeast and parsley, if desired.

LOW-CARB TACO SOUP

Prep: 0 mins

Cook: 20 mins

Total: 20 mins*

Yield: 8 servings

Nutritional info per serving:

Calories	*Carbs*	*Protein*	*Fat*
227	*7g*	*17g*	*14g*

INGREDIENTS:

1lb grass-fed ground beef

3 T taco seasoning

4 cups beef bone broth (recipe page 1), divided

2 (14.5oz) cans diced tomatoes with liquid

¾ cup Paleo Ranch Dressing such as Primal Kitchen

***Optional:** ½ cup chopped cilantro*

METHOD:

Select "Saute" on your Instant Pot, and brown the ground beef until no longer pink (about 8 minutes). Add the taco seasoning and ⅓ cup of the broth. Simmer, stirring occasionally until the broth is mostly gone (about 2 minutes). Press "Cancel."

Add the remaining broth and diced tomatoes, and stir to combine.

Secure the lid on the Instant Pot and move the vent knob to the sealed position. Select "Manual" and cook on high pressure for 3 minutes. When the cooking time is up, move the vent knob to "Venting" to release the pressure quickly.

Stir in the ranch dressing and serve topped with cilantro.

CREAMY CAULIFLOWER SOUP

Prep: 5 mins

Cook: 5 mins

Total: 15 mins*

Yield: 4 servings

Nutritional info per serving:

Calories	*Carbs*	*Protein*	*Fat*
145	*10g*	*8g*	*9g*

INGREDIENTS:

1 medium head cauliflower, cut into florets

1 small onion, roughly chopped

4 cloves garlic, chopped

2 cups chicken bone broth (recipe page 3)

1 T lemon juice

½ cup full-fat coconut milk

¼ t allspice

2 T ghee, optional

Sea salt and ground black pepper, to taste

***Optional garnishes:** chopped chives, black pepper, paprika, crumbled bacon*

METHOD:

Place the cauliflower, onion, garlic, broth, lemon juice, and allspice in the bowl of the Instant Pot.

Secure the lid and move the vent knob to the sealed position. Select "Manual" and cook on high pressure for 5 minutes. Let the pressure release naturally for 5 minutes and then carefully move the vent knob to "Venting" to release the rest of the pressure.

Press "Cancel" and remove the lid.

Add the ghee (if using) and the coconut milk. Using an immersion blender, puree the soup until smooth and creamy. Alternatively, you can puree the soup in a blender.

Serve hot, topped with your favorite garnishes.

Mains.

CHICKEN CACCIATORE

Prep: 10 mins

Cook: 11 mins

Total: 21 mins*

Yield: 4 servings

Nutritional info per serving:

Calories	*Carbs*	*Protein*	*Fat*
199	*10g*	*8g*	*9g*

INGREDIENTS:

1¼ lbs chicken breasts

1 t sea salt

¼ t black pepper

2 cloves garlic, minced

1 small onion, diced

1 medium red bell pepper, diced

1 (14.5 oz) can diced tomatoes, including liquid

1 T fresh rosemary, chopped

1 T fresh thyme, chopped

1 medium bay leaf

½ cup water

METHOD:

Season the chicken breasts on both sides with salt and pepper. Place the chicken into the Instant Pot.

In a medium bowl, stir together the garlic, onion, bell peppers, diced tomatoes plus their liquid, rosemary, thyme, and water. Pour the sauce evenly over the chicken. Place a bay leaf in the center.

Place the lid on the Instant pot and lock it in place. Move the vent knob to the sealed position. Select "Manual" and cook on high pressure for 11 minutes.

Use either the quick release or natural release and remove the lid.

Serve right away.

***Tip:** If you prefer a thicker sauce, remove the chicken and cook the sauce on "Saute" mode until it cooks down to your liking.

DA ROM
T.226

HERBED CHICKEN AND BRUSSELS SPROUTS

Prep: 20 mins

Cook: 40 mins

Total: 1 hr*

Yield: 6 servings

Nutritional info per serving:

Calories	Carbs	Protein	Fat
339	10g	32g	18g

INGREDIENTS:

2 t sea salt

2 t paprika

2 t dried thyme

½ t black pepper

2 lbs bone-in chicken parts, organic free-range

2 T ghee or avocado oil

1 medium red onion, sliced into rounds

1 lb Brussels sprouts

4 cloves garlic, whole

½ cup broth or water

1½ t Dijon mustard

METHOD:

In a small bowl, combine the sea salt, paprika, dried thyme, and black pepper.

Rub the chicken with the salt mixture. Be sure to use all of it.

Select the "Saute" function on the Instant Pot. Melt the ghee or avocado oil in the pot.

Add the chicken pieces and cook, undisturbed for 5–7 minutes until the skin starts to brown. Using tongs or two long-handled cooking spoons, turn the chicken over and cook for another 5 minutes.

Press the "Cancel" button to stop sauteing. Lift the chicken from the pot and add the onion, Brussels sprouts, garlic, and broth or water.

Put the chicken on top of the vegetables.

Place the lid on the Instant Pot and lock it in place. Move the vent knob to the sealed position.

Select "Manual" and cook on high pressure for 12 minutes.

When the cooking time is done, allow the pressure to release naturally for 15 minutes, and then carefully move the vent knob to "Venting" to release the rest of the pressure. Press "Cancel."

Remove the chicken, plate it on a serving dish, and arrange the vegetables around the chicken, leaving the juices in the pot.

Press saute and bring the juices to a simmer.

Add the mustard, and simmer to reduce the sauce by half (about 10 minutes).

Pour the sauce over the chicken and vegetables, and serve hot!

LEMON CHICKEN WITH CAULIFLOWER MASH

Prep: 5 mins

Cook: 25 mins

Total: 30 mins*

Yield: 4 servings

Nutritional info per serving:

Calories	*Carbs*	*Protein*	*Fat*
363	*4g*	*25g*	*26g*

INGREDIENTS:

2 T avocado oil

4 (1¼ lbs) chicken thighs, bone-in, skin-on

1 small onion, chopped

2 cloves garlic, minced

1 t dried thyme or 1T fresh, chopped

1 t dried rosemary or 1T fresh, chopped

¾ cup chicken bone broth (recipe page 3)

1 lemon, juice only

1 T coconut flour

2 T full-fat coconut milk

Sea salt and pepper, to taste

***Optional:** 1 T ghee*

METHOD:

Add the avocado oil to the Instant Pot and select "Saute." When the oil is hot but not smoking, add the chicken thighs, skin side down, and cook until crisp and golden (about 6 minutes). With tongs or a spatula, turn the chicken over and cook for 6 more minutes until browned on the other side. Remove the chicken from the pot and set aside.

Add the onion, garlic, thyme, sea salt, pepper, and rosemary to the drippings in the pot and saute until fragrant (about 1–2 minutes). Add the bone broth and lemon juice. Using a spatula, scrape the browned bits off the bottom of the pot. Press "Cancel."

Place the chicken back in the Instant Pot and secure the lid. Move the vent knob to the sealed position, and select "Manual." Cook for 12 minutes on high pressure.

While the chicken is cooking, stir the coconut flour into the coconut milk until it is dissolved. Set aside.

When the cooking time is up, carefully move the vent knob to "Venting" to quickly release the pressure. Press "Cancel."

Remove the chicken from the pot and select "Saute." Stir the coconut flour mixture into the sauce in the pot and simmer until thickened (about 2 minutes). Stir in ghee (if using).

Serve chicken with cauliflower mashed potatoes (recipe page 7) and sauce spooned over the chicken.

BARBACOA BEEF

Prep: 10 mins

Cook: 1 hr 10 mins

Total: 1 hr 20 mins*

Yield: 8 servings

Nutritional info per serving:

Calories	*Carbs*	*Protein*	*Fat*
462	*10g*	*31g*	*34g*

INGREDIENTS:

1 T avocado oil

2 lb beef brisket or chuck roast

½ cup beef bone broth (recipe page 1)

2 medium chipotle chiles in adobo sauce (including the sauce, about 4t)

5 cloves garlic, minced

2 T apple cider vinegar

2 T lime juice

1 T dried oregano

2 t cumin

2 t sea salt

1 t black pepper

½ t ground cloves, optional

2 whole bay leaves

METHOD:

Trim and cut the brisket or chuck roast in half to fit the pot.

Select "Saute" mode and brown the brisket on all sides in the oil (about 3–4 minutes). You may have to do each piece of brisket separately.

While the beef is browning, combine the broth, chipotle chiles in adobo sauce, garlic, apple cider vinegar, lime juice, dried oregano, cumin, sea salt, black pepper, and ground cloves in a blender. Purée until smooth.

After all of the beef is browned, press "Cancel" and place all the brisket in the Instant Pot. Pour the puréed mixture from the blender on top. Turn the brisket over in the sauce to make sure all the surfaces are coated. Add the bay leaves.

Place the lid on the Instant Pot and lock it in place. Move the vent knob to the sealed position.

Select "Manual" and cook on high pressure for 1 hour until the beef is tender.

Carefully turn the vent knob to "Venting" for quick pressure release, or release the pressure naturally, while keeping the Instant Pot on warm mode.

Remove the lid and discard the bay leaves.

Shred the meat using two forks, and stir into the juices.

BEEF SHORT RIBS

Prep: 10 mins

Cook: 45 mins

Total: 55 mins*

Yield: 4 servings

Nutritional info per serving:

Calories	Carbs	Protein	Fat
342	3g	34g	21g

INGREDIENTS:

2 cups beef bone broth (recipe page 1)

2 T coconut aminos

1 T tomato paste

1 t minced garlic

1½ lbs grass-fed boneless beef short ribs

½ t sea salt

¼ t black pepper

1 T ghee, or cooking fat of choice

1 sprig fresh rosemary

***Optional:** 2 green onions, chopped*

METHOD:

In a small bowl, stir the broth, coconut aminos, tomato paste, and garlic together until combined. Set aside.

Blot the short ribs dry with a paper towel, and season with salt and pepper.

Select "Saute" mode on the Instant Pot and brown the short ribs on all sides in the ghee.

Press "Cancel" and pour the broth mixture over the short ribs. Place the rosemary on top of the meat.

Secure the lid on the Instant Pot and lock it in place. Move the vent knob to the sealed position.

Select "Manual" and cook on high pressure for 45 minutes. Once the time is up, let the pressure release naturally.

Serve with cauliflower mashed potatoes (recipe page 5) and spoon the broth over the short ribs. Garnish with green onions, if desired.

BROWN
WELL
WILD
SLOW COOK
SAUTE
RICE/RISOTTO
BEANS/LENTILS
STEAM

PORK CHILI

Prep: 5 mins

Cook: 20 mins

Total: 25 mins*

Yield: 4 servings

*Nutritional info per serving:***

Calories	Carbs	Protein	Fat
347	8g	21g	24g

INGREDIENTS:

1 T avocado oil

½ cup finely chopped onion

1 lb ground pork

½ t salt + extra to taste

½ t pepper + extra to taste

2 cups crushed tomatoes

6 garlic cloves, minced

3 T smoked paprika

1T ground cumin

½ T chipotle powder

Avocado cream

½ cup coconut milk

1 lime

1 avocado

***Optional:** Garnish with lime wedges, pickled veggies (recipe page 13), and chopped chives.*

***Nutritional values do not include avocado cream*

METHOD:

Select "Saute" mode on the Instant Pot and heat the avocado oil until warm, but not smoking.

Add the onion and saute until starting to sweat (about 1–2 minutes).

Add the pork and season with salt and pepper. Saute, stirring occasionally, until cooked through (about 5 – 6 minutes). Press "Cancel."

Add the tomatoes, garlic, paprika, cumin, and chipotle powder, and stir to combine.

Place the lid on the Instant Pot and lock it in place. Move the vent knob to the sealed position.

Select "Manual" or "Pressure Cook" and cook on high pressure for 5 minutes.

Once the cooking time is up, carefully move the vent knob to open for a quick steam release.

Optional: While the chili is cooking, combine the avocado, lime juice, and coconut milk in a blender and process until smooth.

Scoop the chili into a bowl, and top with avocado cream, lime wedges, pickled veggies (recipe page 13), and chives as desired.

STUFFED PEPPERS

Prep: 10 mins

Cook: 18 mins

Total: 28 mins*

Yield: 6 servings

Nutritional info per serving:

Calories	*Carbs*	*Protein*	*Fat*
244	*10g*	*25g*	*12g*

INGREDIENTS:

1 T avocado oil

1 lb ground turkey

¼ cup finely chopped onion

1¾ cups raw cauliflower rice

1 t paprika

1 t sea salt

½ t black pepper

¼ t ground cumin

1 small tomato, chopped

½ cup water

1 t oregano

4 medium bell peppers

***Optional:** 1 T chopped parsley for garnish*

METHOD:

Select "Saute" mode on the Instant Pot and heat the avocado oil until warm, but not smoking. Add the turkey and onion and cook until the turkey is no longer pink (about 5 minutes).

Add the cauliflower rice, tomato, water, and seasonings and cook. Stir occasionally until the mixture is warmed through and starts to thicken (about 5 minutes).

While the mixture is cooking, cut the tops off the peppers, and remove the seeds.

When the mixture is ready, press "Cancel" and fill the peppers with equal portions of the mixture, using all of it to make mounds on the tops of the peppers. Set aside.

Pour 1½ cups water into the pot and place a steamer rack or trivet on the bottom.

Place the stuffed peppers on the rack.

Secure the lid on the Instant Pot and move the vent knob to the sealed position.

Select "Manual" and cook on high pressure for 8 minutes. When the cooking time is up, carefully move the vent knob to "Venting" to release the pressure quickly.

Carefully remove the peppers from the pot and garnish with parsley, if desired

ITALIAN MEATBALLS

Prep: 10 mins

Cook: 25 mins

Total: 35 mins*

Yield: 5 servings

Nutritional info per serving:

Calories	Carbs	Protein	Fat
332	7g	32g	19g

INGREDIENTS:

1½ lbs ground beef

2 T fresh parsley, chopped

½ cup almond flour

2 eggs

1 t sea salt

1 t dried onion flakes

¼ t black pepper

¼ t garlic powder

¼ t dried oregano

⅓ cup water

2 T avocado oil, or coconut oil

3 cups marinara sauce, no added sugar

METHOD:

In a large bowl, with your hands, mix the ground beef, parsley, almond flour, eggs, salt, onion flakes, pepper, garlic powder, oregano, and water until combined.

Form into 20 meatballs, approximately 2-inches in diameter. Set aside.

Place the avocado oil in the Instant Pot and select "Saute." When the oil is hot but not smoking, sear 6–7 meatballs at a time, until browned on the tops and bottoms (about 2 minutes per side).*

When all of the meatballs are seared, press "Cancel" and place all of the meatballs back in the bowl of the Instant Pot, layering them, leaving ½-inch space between them.

Pour the marinara sauce over the top.

Secure the Instant Pot lid and select "Manual." Cook on low pressure for 10 minutes.

When the cooking time is up, carefully move the vent knob to "Venting" to quickly release the pressure.

Serve your meatballs with spaghetti squash (recipe page 9) or zucchini noodles (recipe page 11).

*Alternatively, for the ease of cooking on a flat surface, you can saute your meatballs in a pan on the stove and then transfer them back to the Instant Pot.

BRAISED LAMB SHANKS WITH PINE NUTS

Prep: 5 mins

Cook: 55 mins

Total: 1 hr*

Yield: 4 servings

Nutritional info per serving:

Calories	*Carbs*	*Protein*	*Fat*
366	*7g*	*21g*	*29g*

INGREDIENTS:

½ t sea salt

¼ t black pepper

2 T coconut flour

4 bone-in lamb shanks (about 3½ lbs)

3 T avocado oil

1 cup chicken bone broth (recipe page 3)

4 dill sprigs + 1½T finely-chopped dill for garnish

½ medium onion, diced

2 garlic cloves, thinly sliced

1 small lemon, sliced, seeds picked out

1 T freshly squeezed lemon juice

½ cup toasted pine nuts

Sauteed cauliflower rice, for serving (recipe page 5)

METHOD:

In a small bowl, combine the salt, pepper, and coconut flour, and mix to combine.

Place the lamb shanks on a plate and sprinkle the coconut flour mixture all over the lamb until the shanks are coated on all sides.

Select "Saute" on the Instant Pot and sear the coated lamb shanks in the avocado oil, 2 at a time, until they are browned, 2–3 minutes per side. Set the seared lamb shanks aside.

Add the onion and garlic to the pot and stir constantly until the onion starts to soften (about 1 minute). "Press Cancel" and add the lamb shanks back to the pot.

Pour in the bone broth and place the lemon slices and dill sprigs on top of the shanks.

Secure the lid and move the vent knob to the sealed position.

Select "Manual" and cook on high pressure for 45 minutes. When the cooking time is up, let the pressure release naturally for 15 minutes and then move the vent knob to "Venting" to release the remaining pressure quickly.

Press "Cancel" and transfer the shanks to shallow bowls, keep warm.

Select "Saute" and stir in the lemon juice and 1 tablespoon of the chopped dill to the pot. Let the sauce come to a boil and reduce for 2–3 minutes.

Spoon the sauce along with the onion and lemon slices over the lamb shanks.

Sprinkle with the pine nuts and the remaining ½ tablespoon of chopped dill, and serve with cauliflower rice. Enjoy!

KETO GUMBO

Prep: 10 mins

Cook: 20 mins

Total: 30 mins*

Yield: 8 servings

Nutritional info per serving:

Calories	Carbs	Protein	Fat
421	10g	38g	26g

INGREDIENTS:

2 lbs boneless, skinless chicken thighs cut into 1-inch pieces

½ t sea salt

½ t ground pepper

1 T ghee or avocado oil

1 bell pepper, diced

1 onion, diced

2 celery stalks, diced

1 lb fully cooked sausage, cut into rounds

5 cloves fresh garlic, peeled and diced

6 oz tomato paste

1 (15 oz) can diced tomatoes

1–2 cups chicken bone broth (recipe page 3)

1 T Cajun seasoning

¼ t cayenne, or to taste

½ t thyme

½ t oregano

½ lb shrimp, shelled and deveined

METHOD:

Season the chicken pieces with salt and pepper, and set aside. Select "Saute" and sear half the chicken in the ghee on all sides (about 5 minutes). Remove the chicken from the pot, and set aside. Repeat with the remaining half.

When all of the chicken is seared and removed from the pot, add the bell pepper, onion, and celery and saute for 1–2 minutes until the veggies start to sweat. Press "Cancel" and add the chicken back to the pot along with all the remaining ingredients except the shrimp. Stir well to combine.

Secure the Instant Pot lid and move the vent knob to "Sealing."

Select "Manual" and cook the gumbo on high pressure for 5 minutes.

When the cooking time is done, carefully move the vent knob from "Sealing" to "Venting" to quickly release the pressure. Remove the lid and press "Cancel."

Add the shrimp to the pot, select "Saute" and cook for 3–4 minutes until the shrimp are cooked through.

Enjoy!

KETO JAMBALAYA

Prep: 10 mins

Cook: 15 mins

Total: 25 mins*

Yield: 6 servings

Nutritional info per serving:

Calories	*Carbs*	*Protein*	*Fat*
453	*8g*	*37g*	*31g*

INGREDIENTS:

1 T ghee or cooking oil of choice

1 lb boneless, skinless chicken thighs, cut into 1-inch pieces

1 lb fully cooked Andouille sausage, cut into rounds

1 bell pepper, diced

2 celery stalks, sliced

1 small onion, diced

1 (15 oz) can diced tomatoes

¾ cup chicken bone broth (recipe page 3)

3 garlic cloves, peeled and minced

2 bay leaves

1 t salt

1 t garlic powder

1 t paprika

1 t oregano

1 t thyme

½ t pepper

¼ t cayenne or to taste

½ t onion powder

½ lb shrimp, shelled and deveined

1½–2 cups raw cauliflower, riced (recipe page 5)

METHOD:

Select "Saute" on the Instant Pot and sear the chicken in the ghee on all sides, about 5 minutes. Remove the chicken from the pot and set aside.

Place the bell pepper, onion, and celery in the pot and saute for 1–2 minutes until the veggies start to sweat. Press "Cancel" and add the chicken back to the pot along with all of the remaining ingredients except the shrimp. Stir well to combine.

Secure the Instant Pot lid and move the vent knob to "Sealing."

Select "Manual" and cook on high pressure for 5 minutes.

When the cooking time is done, carefully move the vent knob from "Sealing" to "Venting" to quickly release the pressure. Remove the lid and press "Cancel."

Add the shrimp to the pot, select "Saute" and cook for 3–4 minutes until the shrimp are cooked through.

Remove the bay leaves. Serve with cauliflower rice topped with chopped parsley and cilantro (optional).

Enjoy!

SHREDDED CHICKEN TACOS

Prep: 5 mins

Cook: 15 mins

Total: 20 mins*

Yield: 4 servings

*Nutritional info per serving:***

Calories	Carbs	Protein	Fat
419	8g	27g	32g

INGREDIENTS:

Shredded chicken

1½ lb skinless, bone-in, or boneless chicken thighs

1 cup salsa verde

1 T taco seasoning

½ t salt

Avocado crema

1 medium to large avocado, peeled and pitted

½ cup full-fat coconut milk

1 clove garlic peeled

1 T fresh lime juice

½ t sea salt

For the tacos

1 head Bibb lettuce or keto tortillas (recipe page 55)

***Optional:** Top with pico de gallo, thinly sliced radishes, and pickled veggies (recipe page 13).*

***The nutritional information does not include Bibb lettuce or Keto tortillas*

METHOD:

For the shredded chicken: In a medium bowl, mix the salsa and taco seasoning until blended and set aside. Place the chicken in the Instant Pot and add the salsa mixture. Stir to make sure the chicken is covered with the mixture on all sides.

Secure the lid and move the vent knob to "Sealing." Press "Manual" and cook on high pressure for 15 minutes. When the cooking time is done, carefully move the vent knob to "Venting" to quickly release the pressure. Remove the chicken thighs to a medium bowl, and shred using two forks. Return the shredded chicken to the pot and stir it into the salsa.

To make the crema: While the chicken is cooking, combine all ingredients in a food processor or blender. Process until smooth.

To assemble: Spoon the chicken into the keto tortillas or Bibb lettuce wraps, and top with plenty of avocado crema. Finish with fresh pico de gallo, radish slices, and pickled onions and carrots if desired.

NO-BEAN KETO BEEF CHILI

Prep: 5 mins

Cook: 15 mins

Total: 20 mins*

Yield: 6 servings

Nutritional info per serving:

Calories	Carbs	Protein	Fat
263	9g	25g	15g

INGREDIENTS:

1 T avocado oil

1 small onion, diced

½ cup celery, chopped

4 cloves garlic, minced

1½ lb ground beef

1½ t sea salt, or to taste

½ t pepper

2 T chili powder

¼ t cayenne pepper

1 (28 oz) can diced tomatoes

½ cup water

2 T tomato paste

2 bay leaves

½ cup fresh parsley, chopped

METHOD:

Select "Saute" mode and cook the onion and celery, stirring frequently until they are soft and fragrant (about 3 minutes). Stir in the garlic and cook for 1 minute.

Add the beef, season with salt and pepper, and cook until it is almost browned (about 5-6 minutes). Carefully remove the excess fat with a spoon, if desired.

Stir in the chili powder, cayenne, tomatoes, water, and tomato paste and cook for 2-3 more minutes until the mixture starts to bubble.

Add the bay leaves and press "Cancel."

Secure the lid on the Instant Pot and move the vent knob to the sealed position.

Select "Manual" and cook on high pressure for 10 minutes.

Once the cooking time is up, release the steam naturally or carefully move the vent knob to open for a quick steam release.

Scoop the chili into bowls, and garnish with fresh parsley.

CAULIFLOWER MAC AND CHEESE

Prep: 5 mins

Cook: 2 mins

Total: 7 mins*

Yield: 4 servings

Nutritional info per serving:

Calories	*Carbs*	*Protein*	*Fat*
160	*10g*	*7g*	*9g*

INGREDIENTS:

½ cup unsweetened almond milk

¾ cup nutritional yeast, divided

1 T mustard

1 t sea salt

4–6 cups cauliflower florets (1 head of cauliflower)

2 T ghee, melted

***Optional:** ¼ cup scallions*

METHOD:

In a small bowl, stir the almond milk, half the nutritional yeast, mustard, and sea salt.

Add the cauliflower to the Instant Pot and pour the almond milk mixture over the top. Stir in the ghee.

Secure the lid and move the vent knob to the sealed position. Select "Manual" and cook on high pressure for 2 minutes.

When the cooking time is up, carefully move the vent knob to "Venting" and allow the pressure to release quickly.

Let the cauliflower cool slightly, then stir in the remaining nutritional yeast. Serve hot with chopped scallions if desired.

GARLIC CHICKEN WITH ZUCCHINI NOODLES

Prep: 5 mins

Cook: 15 mins

Total: 20 mins*

Yield: 4 servings

Nutritional info per serving:

Calories	*Carbs*	*Protein*	*Fat*
346	*6g*	*21g*	*28g*

INGREDIENTS:

4 (1–1½ lbs) bone-in, skin-on chicken thighs

½ t sea salt

¼ t black pepper

2 T ghee, divided

3 cloves garlic, minced

¼ cup chicken stock

Juice of 1 lemon

Sprig of rosemary, leaves only, chopped

2 zucchini, spiral sliced

METHOD:

Set the Instant Pot to "Saute" and allow it to preheat.

Season the chicken thighs with sea salt and black pepper.

Melt 1 tablespoon of the ghee in the Instant Pot. Add the chicken thighs, skin-side down, two at a time. Brown for 5–7 minutes, or until nicely browned. Press Cancel.

Add all the cooked chicken thighs back to the Instant Pot, and add the remaining ghee, garlic, chicken stock, lemon juice, and rosemary. Lock the lid, close the vent, and set to "Chicken" or "Manual" for 8 minutes.

Allow the pressure to naturally release for 5 minutes, then turn the vent valve and release any remaining pressure before unlocking the lid.

Meanwhile, grease a large skillet with ghee and heat over medium heat. Add the zucchini noodles and saute for about 5 minutes, or until softened.

Add the chicken to the skillet and pour the liquid from the Instant Pot over the top. Serve hot and enjoy!

DAIRY-FREE BEEF STROGANOFF

Prep: 10 mins

Cook: 30 mins

Total: 40 mins*

Yield: 4 servings

Nutritional info per serving:

Calories	Carbs	Protein	Fat
371	10g	28g	24g

INGREDIENTS:

1 T avocado oil

1 medium onion, diced

2 slices bacon, diced

2 cloves garlic, chopped

1 lb beef stew meat, or sirloin, cut into 1-inch cubes

1 t paprika

3 T tomato paste

2½ cups button mushrooms, sliced

1 cup beef bone broth (recipe page 1)

Sea salt and pepper, to taste

METHOD:

Select "Saute" mode on the Instant Pot and heat the avocado oil until warm, but not smoking.

Add the onion and bacon, and cook until bacon is cooked, but not browned.

Add the garlic and the beef, and brown beef on all sides (about 2 minutes).

Stir in the paprika, tomato paste, mushrooms, and broth. Season with salt and pepper.

Secure the lid on the Instant Pot and move the vent knob to the sealed position.

Select "Manual" and cook on high pressure for 30 minutes.

Once the cooking time is up, release steam naturally or carefully move the vent knob to open for a quick steam release.

INSTANT POT BUTTER CHICKEN

Prep: 10 mins

Cook: 15 mins

Total: 25 mins*

Yield: 8 servings

Nutritional info per serving:

Calories	Carbs	Protein	Fat
222	7g	20g	12g

INGREDIENTS:

1¼ t ground ginger

1 t garam masala

1 t chili powder

1 t cumin

1 t turmeric powder

1 t sea salt

¼ t black pepper

2 lbs chicken thighs, skinless, boneless, cut into bite-sized pieces

2 T ghee

1 medium onion, chopped

4 cloves garlic, minced

1(15 oz) can tomato puree

½ cup full-fat coconut milk

Fresh cilantro leaves, for garnish

METHOD:

In a large bowl, mix the ginger, garam masala, chili powder, cumin, turmeric, salt, and pepper until combined. Add the chicken pieces and stir to combine until the chicken is coated on all sides. Set aside.

Select "Saute" on the Instant Pot, and melt the ghee. Add the onion and garlic and cook, stirring occasionally until translucent (about 3 minutes).

Add the chicken and cook until all sides are starting to brown (about 5 minutes). Stir in the tomato sauce, and press "Cancel."

Secure the Instant Pot lid and move the vent knob to the sealed position. Select "Manual" and cook on high pressure for 8 minutes. Carefully move the vent knob to "Venting" to release the pressure quickly.

Open the lid and stir in the coconut milk. Serve topped with cilantro leaves.

INSTANT POT CARNITAS

Prep: 10 mins

Cook: 45 mins

Total: 55 mins*

Yield: 6 servings

Nutritional info per serving:

Calories	*Carbs*	*Protein*	*Fat*
243	*6g*	*29g*	*10g*

INGREDIENTS:

1 T avocado oil or healthy cooking fat

2 lbs Boston butt or pork shoulder

2 t sea salt

½ t ground black pepper

1 orange, halved

1 cup water

2 limes, juiced

1 jalapeno, seeded and diced

1½ t onion powder

3 cloves garlic, minced

1 t paprika

1 t dried parsley

½ t cumin

***Optional:** fresh cilantro leaves, lime wedges, chopped onion*

METHOD:

Cut the pork into 3 or 4 chunks. Season with salt and pepper, and set aside.

Select "saute" on the Instant Pot and heat the oil until hot, but not smoking. Add the pork in batches as needed, and sear 3-5 minutes on each side until browned. Press "Cancel."

Add all the meat back to the Instant Pot, and squeeze in the orange juice. Add the orange rind to the pot along with the water, lime juice, jalapeno, onion powder, garlic, paprika, parsley, and cumin. Stir to combine the ingredients.

Secure the Instant Pot lid and move the vent knob to the sealed position. Select "Meat" or "Manual" and cook for 30 minutes on high pressure. When the cooking time is done, let the pressure release naturally.

Remove the lid and shred the pork with 2 forks.

Serve with desired toppings or make carnitas tacos with Keto Tortillas (recipe page 15)

Optional: For crispy carnitas, place the shredded pork on a baking tray with a few tablespoons of sauce and broil in the oven for 3-5 minutes until the edges start to brown and crisp.

CHINESE CASHEW CHICKEN

Prep: 10 mins

Cook: 20 mins

Total: 25 mins*

Yield: 6 servings

Nutritional info per serving:

Calories	*Carbs*	*Protein*	*Fat*
297	*10g*	*28g*	*15g*

INGREDIENTS:

1 T sesame oil

½ cup coconut aminos

3 T sugar-free ketchup, such as Primal Kitchen

2 T apple cider vinegar

3 T freshly squeezed orange juice

6 cloves garlic, minced (about 1T)

1-inch piece fresh ginger, minced (about 1T)

½ t Chinese Five Spice powder

½ t red pepper flakes, or to taste

1½ lbs chicken breasts, boneless, skinless, cut into bite-sized pieces

1 T avocado oil, or coconut oil

2 T coconut flour, divided

¼ t sea salt

¼ t ground black pepper

3 T water

¾ cup cashews

***Optional:** chopped green onion, sesame seeds*

METHOD:

In a medium bowl, combine the sesame oil, coconut aminos, ketchup, vinegar, orange juice, garlic, ginger, Chinese Five Spice powder, and red pepper flakes. Set aside.

In another bowl, toss the chicken pieces with 1 tablespoon of the coconut flour, salt, and pepper.

Select "Saute" on the Instant Pot and heat the avocado oil until hot, but not smoking. Add the chicken in batches as needed, and sear until the pieces start to brown (about 5 minutes per batch). Press "Cancel."

Place all of the chicken back into the Instant Pot and stir in the sauce.

Secure the Instant Pot lid and move the vent knob to the sealed position. Select "Manual" and cook on high pressure for 10 minutes.

While the chicken is cooking, mix the remaining tablespoon of coconut flour with the water. Set aside.

When the cooking time is done, carefully move the vent knob to "Venting" to release the pressure quickly. Press "Cancel"

Remove the lid and stir in the coconut flour slurry. Select "Saute" and add the cashews.

Cook, stirring occasionally until the sauce has thickened, about 2 minutes.

Serve topped with chopped green onion and sesame seeds over Cauliflower Rice, if desired (recipe page 5).

Dessert.

MOLTEN CHOCOLATE LAVA CAKE

Prep: 10 mins

Cook: 10 mins

Total: 20 mins*

Yield: 4 servings

Nutritional info per serving:

Calories	Carbs	Protein	Fat
333	10g	6g	29g

INGREDIENTS:

6 T melted coconut oil plus extra for greasing

3 eggs

½ cup unsweetened almond milk

2 t vanilla extract

⅔ cup almond flour

2 T Lakanto monk fruit powder

2 T raw cacao powder

1½ t cream of tartar

¾ t baking soda

¾ t arrowroot powder

¼ cup sugar-free dark chocolate chips

1½ cups water

METHOD:

Lightly grease 4 (6-ounce) heat-safe ramekins with coconut oil.

In a large mixing bowl, whisk together the eggs, almond milk, melted coconut oil, and vanilla extract until combined.

Into the wet ingredients, sift the almond flour, monk fruit powder, cacao powder, cream of tartar, baking soda, and arrowroot powder. Whisk just until a smooth batter forms.

Stir in the chocolate chips.

Divide the mixture evenly among the 4 ramekins, filling them until ¾ full. Pour the water into the Instant Pot bowl and set a steamer rack or trivet in the bottom. Place three ramekins on the rack, and one on top of the three, in the center.

Secure the lid on the Instant Pot and move the vent knob to the sealed position.

Select "Manual" and cook on high pressure for 10 minutes.

Once the cooking time is up, carefully move the knob to "Venting" to quickly release the pressure.

The ramekins will be hot and slippery, so wear oven mitts to remove them from the Instant Pot.

(Don't be concerned if there is a little extra liquid around the ramekin rims when you open the Instant Pot. It will absorb into the cakes in a minute or two.) Serve immediately in ramekins or scooped onto plates while still warm and molten.

LEMON CHEESECAKE

Prep: 10 mins

Cook: 20 mins

Chill: 2 hrs

Total: 2 hrs 30 mins*

Yield: 8 servings

Nutritional info per serving:

Calories	*Carbs*	*Protein*	*Fat*
203	*0g*	*5g*	*19g*

INGREDIENTS:

1½ cups water

Coconut oil for greasing the pan

16 oz non-dairy or regular cream cheese, room temperature

¾ t pure monk fruit sweetener

2 eggs, room temperature

2 t vanilla extract

Zest of 1 lemon

Optional: 2 drops lemon extract

METHOD:

Pour the water into the Instant Pot bowl and set a steamer rack or trivet in the bottom.

Wrap a piece of foil around the bottom of a 6- or 7-inch springform pan to prevent water from getting into the pan and the cheesecake from seeping out. (You can also use a heat-proof dish.) Grease the inside of the pan with coconut oil.

In a medium-size bowl, beat the cream cheese and sweetener until smooth and creamy (about 2 minutes).

Add the eggs, vanilla, lemon zest, and lemon extract (if using), and beat briefly until combined.

Transfer the mixture to the springform pan and place it on the steamer rack in the Instant Pot.

Secure the lid and move the vent knob to the sealed position.

Select "Manual" and cook for 20 minutes. Once the cooking time is up, release the steam naturally.

Dab any moisture on top of the cake with a paper towel.

Refrigerate the cheesecake for at least 2 hours before removing from the springform pan prior to serving.

Cut into slices and serve chilled.

VANILLA CUSTARD

Prep: 5 mins

Cook: 9 mins

Chill: 3 hrs

Total: 3 hrs 14 mins*

Yield: 4 servings

Nutritional info per serving:

Calories	Carbs	Protein	Fat
216	2g	4g	20g

INGREDIENTS:

1 large egg + 2 egg yolks

2 t vanilla extract

¼ t pure monk fruit powder

*1¾ cups canned coconut cream***

***Optional:** Garnish with fresh ground nutmeg*

***Note:** We recommend Trader Joes or Whole Foods canned coconut cream.*

METHOD:

In a medium bowl, whisk the eggs, vanilla, monk fruit powder, and coconut cream until combined.

Divide the mixture evenly among 4 (6-ounce) ramekins, filling them until ¾ full. Cover with foil. Pour 1½ cups water into the Instant Pot bowl and set a steamer rack or trivet in the bottom. Place three ramekins on the rack, and one on top of the three, in the center.

Secure the lid on the Instant Pot and lock it in place. Move the vent knob to the sealed position.

Select "Manual" and cook on high pressure for 9 minutes. Once the cooking time is up, carefully move the vent knob to "Venting" to quickly release the pressure.

The ramekins will be hot and slippery, so wear oven mitts or use a towel to remove them from the Instant Pot.

Cool to room temperature (about 1 hour), then place in the fridge to chill for at least 2 hours.

Just before serving, garnish with a dash of fresh ground nutmeg if desired.

CHOCOLATE CUSTARD

Prep: 10 mins

Cook: 7 mins

Chill: 3 hrs

Total: 3 hrs 17 mins*

Yield: 4 servings

Nutritional info per serving:

Calories	*Carbs*	*Protein*	*Fat*
214	*7g*	*3g*	*18g*

INGREDIENTS:

1¾ cups (1 can) full-fat coconut milk, divided

1 T arrowroot powder

Ghee or coconut oil for greasing ramekins.

*⅓ cup unsweetened chocolate baking chips***

¼ t vanilla

¼ t pure monk fruit powder

1 T cacao powder

2 eggs, beaten

***Optional:** Whipped coconut cream*

*****Note:** We recommend Lily's unsweetened baking chips.*

METHOD:

Grease 4 ramekins with ghee or coconut oil, and set aside.

Combine ¼ cup coconut milk and the arrowroot starch in a small bowl, and whisk until completely combined. Add it to the remaining coconut milk in a medium saucepan, and heat over medium heat.

When the mixture begins to bubble and thicken (about 2 minutes), remove it from the heat and add all the remaining ingredients, except for the eggs. Stir constantly until the mixture is smooth and the chocolate chips are melted and combined. (If the mixture remains a bit grainy in appearance, it won't affect the finished custard's taste or texture.) Once the mixture has cooled slightly (about 5 minutes), add the eggs and whisk well until they are completely combined.

Divide the mixture evenly among the 4 ramekins, filling them until ¾ full. Pour 1½ cups water into the Instant Pot bowl and set a steamer rack or trivet in the bottom. Place three ramekins on the rack, and one on top of the three, in the center.

Secure the lid on the Instant Pot and lock it in place. Move the vent knob to the sealed position.

Select "Manual" and cook on high pressure for 9 minutes. Once the cooking time is up, carefully move the vent knob to "Venting" to quickly release the pressure.

The ramekins will be hot and slippery, so wear oven mitts or use a towel to remove them from the Instant Pot.

Cool to room temperature (about 1 hour), then place in the fridge to chill completely (at least 2 hours).

Top with coconut whipped cream and a dash of sea salt and enjoy!

CHOCOLATE FUDGE CAKE

Prep: 5 mins

Cook: 40 mins

Total: 50 mins*

Yield: 8 servings

Nutritional info per serving:

Calories	*Carbs*	*Protein*	*Fat*
191	*9g*	*7g*	*17g*

INGREDIENTS:

Coconut oil for greasing pan

1 cup almond flour

1 cup cacao powder

½ t baking soda

½ t sea salt

1t pure monk fruit powder

¾ cup full-fat coconut milk

2 T coconut oil, melted

2 eggs

1 t vanilla extract

METHOD:

Grease a 6-inch heat-proof baking dish or springform pan with coconut oil, and line the bottom with parchment paper. If using a springform pan, wrap a sheet of foil around the bottom to prevent the cake batter from leaking out, and water from leaking in. Place a steamer rack or trivet in the Instant Pot bowl, and add 1½ cups water.

In a medium bowl, mix the almond flour, cacao powder, baking soda, salt, and monk fruit powder until combined. Set aside.

In another medium bowl, beat the eggs and stir in the coconut milk, coconut oil, and vanilla. Add the dry ingredients and mix just until combined (the batter will be thick, like brownie batter.)

Pour the mixture into the prepared cake pan, cover the top with foil, and place it on top of the rack in the Instant Pot.

Secure the lid and move the vent knob to the sealed position.

Select "Manual" and cook on high pressure for 40 minutes. Once the cooking time is up, let the steam release naturally for 10 minutes then carefully move the vent knob to "Venting" to release the rest of the pressure.

Lift the cake from the Instant Pot, remove the foil covering the top, and cool on a rack for 10–15 minutes before serving.

CARROT CAKE

Prep: 15 mins

Cook: 50 mins

Total: 1 hr 5 mins*

Yield: 8 servings

Nutritional info per serving:

Calories	Carbs	Protein	Fat
220	10g	5g	21g

INGREDIENTS:

Bottom cake layer

¾ cup almond flour

1 T coconut flour

⅛ t baking soda

1 t cinnamon

¼ t allspice

2½ T coconut oil, melted, plus more for greasing the pan

2½ T Lakanto Monkfruit Sweetener Classic

2 large eggs at room temperature

1 T almond milk or coconut milk

½ t vanilla extract

1 t lemon juice

¼ cup grated carrot

METHOD:

To make the bottom cake layer: Preheat the oven to 350°F and grease a 6- or 7-inch springform pan with coconut oil. Wrap the bottom with foil to prevent spillage. Set aside.

In a medium bowl, combine the almond flour, coconut flour, baking soda, cinnamon, and allspice. Set aside.

In a large bowl, using a hand mixer, mix the coconut oil and sweetener until combined. Add the eggs, almond milk, and vanilla, and beat just until combined.

Add the dry ingredients and mix just until combined. Gently fold in the carrots.

Transfer the batter to the prepared pan and bake for 20 minutes, or until a toothpick inserted into the center comes out clean. Allow to cool to the touch before adding the cheesecake layer. While the cake is cooling, make the cheesecake layer.

Note: The bottom layer can be made ahead and refrigerated or frozen until ready to use.

continued on pg 119.

CARROT CAKE

continued...

INGREDIENTS:

Cheesecake layer

8 oz dairy-free or regular cream cheese, softened

3 T Lakanto Monkfruit Sweetener Classic

1t vanilla extract

¼ cup dairy-free or regular sour cream

¼ cup coconut cream or full-fat coconut milk

1 large egg

Topping (Optional)

1 oz dairy-free or regular cream cheese, softened

¼ t vanilla extract

1 T coconut cream or full-fat coconut milk

1 T Lakanto Powdered Monkfruit Sweetener

¼ cup chopped walnuts

METHOD:

To make the cheesecake layer: In a large bowl, using a hand mixer, beat the cream cheese and sweetener until smooth. Add the vanilla, sour cream, coconut cream, and egg, and mix until just combined and smooth in consistency. (Do not overmix.)

Pour the mixture into the pan, over the cooled bottom cake layer and cover securely with foil.

Pour 1½ cups water into the Instant Pot and place a steamer rack or trivet in the bottom. Place the cheesecake on the rack.

Secure the lid on the Instant Pot and move the vent knob to the sealed position.

Select "Manual" and cook on high pressure for 30 minutes. Once the cooking time is up, let the steam release naturally.

Remove the cake from the Instant Pot and leave covered for about 30 minutes before removing the foil. Let it sit for another hour, uncovered before refrigerating it still in the springform pan for 4 hours.

When the time is up, remove the cheesecake from the pan and serve with the optional topping.

To make the optional topping: With a spoon, mix the cream cheese, vanilla, coconut cream, and sweetener in a small bowl. Microwave on high for 10–15 seconds to make the topping pourable. Pour onto the cooled cheesecake and using a knife, spread into a thin layer. Top with walnuts.

CINNAMON ROLLS

Prep: 10 mins

Cook: 20 mins

Chill: 25 mins

Total: 55 mins*

Yield: 8 servings

*Nutritional info per serving:***

Calories	Carbs	Protein	Fat
208	10g	7g	17g

INGREDIENTS:

Dough

1¼ cup blanched almond flour

2 T coconut flour

½ t psyllium husk

1 t baking powder

¼ t sea salt

1 T monk fruit powder

½ t grass-fed beef gelatin dissolved in 2 T warm water

1 T ghee, melted

2 t apple cider vinegar

1 large egg at room temperature

1 egg yolk

Filling

2 T unsalted butter, softened

2 T Lakanto Icing Powder

1½ T ground cinnamon

½ t pure vanilla extract

4 drops liquid Stevia

METHOD:

For the dough: Whisk together the flours, psyllium, baking powder, salt, and monk fruit in a large bowl. In a medium bowl, whisk together the dissolved gelatin, ghee, vinegar, egg, and yolk.

Gradually stir the wet ingredients into the dry. Refrigerate for 15 minutes.

For the filling: Mix together all ingredients in a small bowl and set aside in the fridge.

Roll the dough out between 2 pieces of parchment paper. Spread the cinnamon filling onto the dough, leaving a border of about ¼-inch all the way around. Freeze for 10 minutes.

Transfer to a working space and gently roll the dough off the parchment into a log. Pinch both ends of the log to seal, and slice into eight ½ -inch rolls.

Grease a 7 inch pushpan with ghee, and add the cinnamon rolls. Cover with a paper towel and secure with a piece of aluminum foil on top. Place the trivet inside the Instant Pot, add 2 cups of water, and set the pushpan with the rolls inside. Lock the lid, secure the vent valve, and select "Manual High" for 20 minutes.

To make the icing: In a medium bowl, whisk together the butter, sweetener, and salt. Refrigerate while the cinnamon rolls finish cooking.

When the timer is done, allow the pressure to release before opening the vent valve and unlocking the lid. Use tongs to carefully remove the pan from the pot and frost the cinnamon rolls with the icing while they're still warm.

Frosting (optional)

3 T butter, softened

3 T Lakanto Icing Powder

½ t pure vanilla extract

Pinch of sea salt

KETO CREME BRULEE

Prep: 5 mins

Cook: 9 mins

Chill: 2 hrs

Rest: 1 hr

Total: 3 hrs 14 mins*

Yield: 4 servings

Nutritional info per serving:

Calories	Carbs	Protein	Fat
257	6g	6g	23g

INGREDIENTS:

Creme brulee

6 egg yolks

1 T vanilla extract

¼ t + ⅛ t pure monk fruit powder

*1¾ cups canned coconut cream***

Topping

3 t keto sweetener that resembles sugar such as Lakanto classic, divided

***Note:** *We recommend Trader Joes or Whole Foods canned coconut cream.*

METHOD:

For the creme brulee: In a medium bowl, whisk the egg yolks, vanilla, monk fruit powder, and coconut cream until combined.

Divide the mixture evenly among 4 (6-ounce) ramekins, filling them until ¾ full. Cover with foil. Pour 1½ cups water into the Instant Pot bowl, and set a steamer rack or trivet in the bottom. Place three ramekins on the rack, and one on top of the three, in the center.

Secure the lid on the Instant Pot and lock it in place. Move the vent knob to the sealed position.

Select "Manual" and cook on high pressure for 9 minutes. Once the cooking time is up, let the steam release naturally for 10 minutes, and then open the vent to release the remaining pressure.

Remove the ramekins from the Instant Pot and take off the foil.

Cool to room temperature (about 1 hour), then place in the fridge to chill for at least 2 hours.

For the creme brulee topping: Place the ramekins on a cookie sheet, and sprinkle ¾ teaspoon of keto topping over each creme brulee. Using a hand torch, burn the sugar until it darkens. Alternatively, you can broil the creme brulees for several minutes until the tops start to darken.

CRUSTLESS PUMPKIN PIE

Prep: 5 mins

Cook: 35 mins

Chill: 2 hrs

Rest: 1 hr

Total: 3 hrs 40 mins*

Yield: 6 servings

Nutritional info per serving:

Calories	*Carbs*	*Protein*	*Fat*
88	*7g*	*3g*	*5g*

INGREDIENTS:

Coconut oil for greasing the pan

2 eggs

½ cup full-fat coconut milk

½ t pure monk fruit powder

1 (15 oz) can pumpkin puree

1 t pumpkin pie spice

1 t vanilla extract

***For the optional topping:** ½ cup whipped coconut cream, cinnamon.*

METHOD:

For the pie: Grease a 6-inch heat-proof bowl or baking pan with 3-inch sides, or a springform pan with coconut oil. Line the bottom with parchment paper. If you're using a springform pan, wrap the bottom and sides with foil to prevent any batter from leaking out and any water from leaking in. Place a trivet or steam rack into the bowl of the Instant Pot and pour in 1½ cups of water.

In a large bowl, whisk the eggs. Add the coconut milk, monk fruit powder, pumpkin, pumpkin pie spice, and vanilla, and whisk until combined. Pour the batter into the prepared pan and place it on the trivet.

Secure the Instant Pot lid and move the vent knob to the sealed position. Select "Manual" and cook on high pressure for 25 minutes. When the cooking time is up, let the pressure release naturally for 10 minutes, and then carefully move the vent knob to "Venting" to release the remaining pressure.

Lift the pan from the bowl and place it on a cooling rack. Remove the foil. Let the pie cool to room temperature for about an hour. Chill in the refrigerator until firm. (About 2 hours for a springform pan and 6-8 hours for a baking pan.) To release the pie, run a knife around the sides. Place a serving plate over the top and flip it over to drop the pie onto the plate. Remove the parchment paper from the pie. Serve with whipped coconut cream.

For the whipped coconut cream: Refrigerate a can of full-fat coconut milk for 2 hours or overnight. Scoop the cream off the top (about ½ cup) and place in a bowl. Add a pinch of cinnamon and whisk briskly until creamy.

index.

B

C

D

P

S

V

Z

DISCOVER MORE PALEO COOKBOOKS

KETO SLOW COOKER COOKBOOK

Imagine coming home at 5 pm and having a fat-burning dinner ready to eat... all you had to do was spend 5-15 minutes that morning throwing it into your crockpot! That's exactly what you get in our brand-new, FREE Keto Slow Cooker Cookbook. Get 80 mouth-watering Keto recipes for breakfast, lunch, dinner, and dessert that keep you in ketosis and help you torch fat. This cookbook is perfect for anyone who is too busy to deal with all the chopping, mixing, cooking, and cleaning of the 5 o'clock scramble. Even busy parents can now get dinner ready for the family—and lose weight—with the Keto Slow Cooker Cookbook. Get yours FREE today!

Get your copy here:

https://paleorecipeteam.com/ketoslowcooker

THE PALEO BREAKFAST BIBLE

Enjoy a variety of delicious, QUICK Paleo Breakfast Recipes (10 minutes or less!). Give yourself a jump-start in the morning with Paleo alternatives to bagels, muffins, and pancakes. Don't be stuck eating eggs and bacon every day—try our apple bread, zesty lemon scones, BBQ chicken egg muffins, and more. With over 100 delicious breakfast recipes, you'll never run out of tasty morning meals!

Get your copy here:

https://www.paleobreakfastrecipes.com/

KETO SWEETS

Enjoy incredible fat-burning "ketofied" recipes like mint chip ice cream, bacon-filled chocolate, and favorites like chocolate chip cookie cake. Each recipe contains no sugar, gluten, processed grains, or soy. They're Paleo-approved, and almost all of them can even be made dairy-free or vegetarian-friendly. Best of all, each one has less than 10 grams of net carbs, so you can stay in ketosis no matter what. With the delicious recipes in *Keto Sweets*, you can FINALLY enjoy your favorite desserts while maintaining ketosis. Get your free copy today (just pay for shipping)!

Get your copy here:

https://paleorecipeteam.com/ketosweets

PALEO SWEETS

Included are 70 delicious, nutritious, Paleo-based desserts you'd swear came from your local bakery! Each of these recipes are all tried, tested, and family approved. Enjoy marveling at all the yummy treats, including mouth-watering brownies, decadent cakes, delicious ice creams, crispy and chewy cookies, perfect pies, and creamy cheesecakes. With the 70 delicious recipes in *Paleo Sweets*, you and your loved ones can FINALLY enjoy your favorite desserts without the downside of traditional desserts. Get your FREE copy HERE (just pay for shipping)!

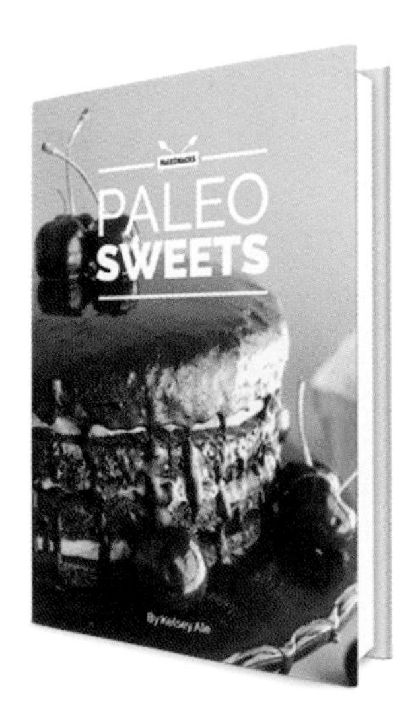

Get your copy here:

https://paleorecipeteam.com/sweets